ŠEVČÍK

OPUS 2 PART 5

SCHOOL OF BOWING
TECHNIQUE

SCHULE DER
BOGENTECHNIK

ÉCOLE DU MÉCANISME
DE L'ARCHET

FOR
CELLO

ARR. FEUILLARD

BOSWORTH

The Works of
OTAKAR ŠEVČÍK

VIOLIN

LITTLE SEVCIK, Elementary Tutor
SEVCIK SCALES & ARPEGGIOS
HOW TO PRACTISE SEVCIK'S MASTERWORKS
INTRODUCTION TO SEVCIK VIOLIN STUDIES
from Op. 1 (by K. W. Rokos)

For More Advanced Pupils

OP. 1. SCHOOL OF VIOLIN TECHNIQUE.
    Part 1. Exercises in the 1st Position.
    Part 2. Exercises in the 2nd-7th Positions.
    Part 3. Exercises in Change of Position.
    Part 4. Exercises in Double-Stopping, Triple-
          Stopping, Quadruple-Stopping (3 & 4-
          part chords). Pizzicato, Flageolet Tones,
          Harmonics.

OP. 1. Complete, bound in Cloth.

Development of the Right Hand

OP. 2. SCHOOL OF BOWING TECHNIQUE.
    (4,000 Exercises in Bowing)
    Parts 1-6
    Exercise Themes to Op. 2.

OP. 3. 40 VARIATIONS
    Piano Accompaniment (optional)

OPS. 2 & 3, Complete, bound in Cloth.

Development of the Left Hand

OP. 6. VIOLIN METHOD FOR BEGINNERS.
    Parts 1-5. 1st Position.
    Part 6.   Studies Preparatory to the various
               Positions.
    Part 7.   5th Position and combining the various
               Positions.

OP. 6. Complete, bound in Cloth.

For Slightly Advanced Pupils

OP. 7. STUDIES PREPARATORY TO THE SHAKE &
    DEVELOPMENT IN DOUBLE-STOPPING.
    Part 1. Exercises in the 1st Position.
    Part 2. Exercises in the 2nd, 3rd, 4th, 5th & 6th
          Positions.

OP. 8. CHANGES OF POSITION & PREPARATORY SCALE
    STUDIES.
    In Thirds, Sixths, Octaves, & Tenths.

OP. 9. PREPARATORY STUDIES IN DOUBLE-STOPPING.
    In Thirds, Sixths, Octaves & Tenths.

OPS. 7, 8 & 9. Complete, bound in Cloth.

VIOLA
Arranged by Lionel Tertis

OP. 1. SCHOOL OF TECHNIQUE.
    Part 1.   Exercises in the 1st Position.
    Part 2.   Exercises in the 2nd-7th Positions.
    Part 3/4. Exercises in Changes of Position & in
            Double, Triple & Quadruple Stopping, etc.

OP. 2. SCHOOL OF BOWING TECHNIQUE.
    Parts 1, 2 & 3.

OP. 3. FORTY VARIATIONS (arr. Margaret Major)
    Piano Accompaniment (optional)

OP. 7. PREPARATORY STUDIES TO THE TRILL
    Part 1.   arr. Alan Arnold; 1st Position
    Part 2.   2nd-6th Position.

OP. 8. CHANGES OF POSITION & PREPARATORY SCALE
    STUDIES.

OP. 9. PREPARATORY STUDIES IN DOUBLE-STOPPING
    (arr. Alan Arnold)

CELLO

OP. 1. THUMB PLACING EXERCISES.
    Part 1.   1st Position (arr. W. Schultz)

OP. 2. SCHOOL OF BOWING TECHNIQUE.
    (4,000 Exercises arr. Feuillard)
    Parts 1-6.

OP. 3. FORTY VARIATIONS (arr. Feuillard)
    Piano Accompaniment (optional)

OP. 8. CHANGES OF POSITION & PREPARATORY SCALE
    STUDIES.
    In Thirds, Sixths, Octaves & Tenths (arr. H. Boyd)

Heft V Uebungen für die Entwickelung der Kraft des Handgelenkes.	Cahier V Exercices pour le développement de la force du poignet. *Ses. V.* *Cvičení směřující k sesílení ohbí ruky.*	Section V Exercises for developing the power of the wrist. Тетрадь V Упражненія для развитія силы кисти

№ 37.

Arpeggien auf drei Saiten. Beispiel mit 1040 Varianten.	Arpèges sur trois cordes. Exemple avec 1040 variantes. *Arpéžie na třech strunách.* *Příklad se 1040 změnami.*	Arpeggios on three strings. Example with 1040 Variations. Арпеджіи на трехъ струнахъ. Примѣръ съ 1040 варіантами.

Edited and translated by H. Brett. Edited by L.R.Feuillard and A.E.Bosworth.

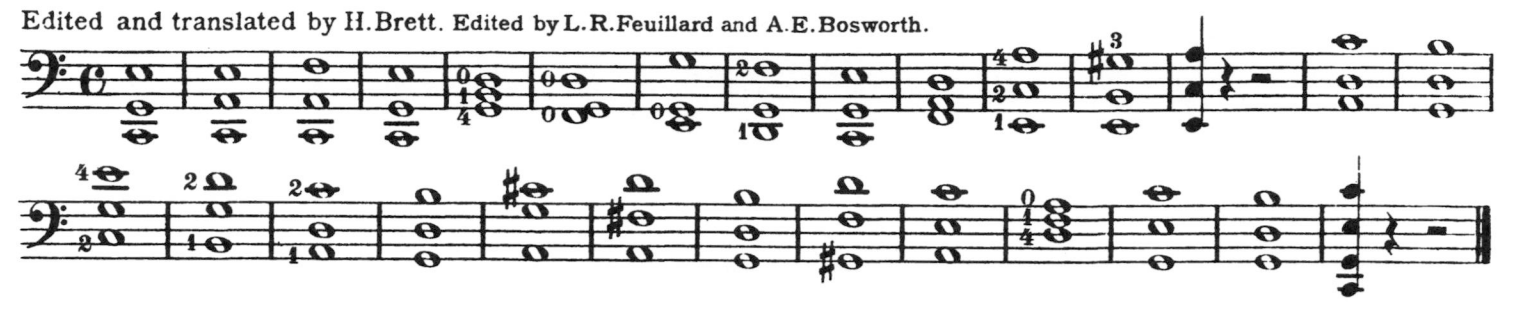

Varianten des vorhergehenden Beispieles. *Změny předešlého příkladu.*	Variantes sur l'exemple précédent.	Variations on the foregoing example. Варіанты предыдущаго примѣра.

Moderato. ♩ = 80.

Die untere Note fängt an. *La note inférieure commence.* The lower note begins. *Dolní notou se počíná.* Нижняя нота начинаетъ.	Die obere Note fängt an. *La note supérieure commence.* The upper note begins. *Vrchní notou se počíná.* Верхняя нота начинаетъ.	Die mittlere Note fängt an. *La note du milieu commence.* The middle note begins. *Střední notou se počíná.* Средняя нота начинаетъ.

Mit ganzem Bogen.
Tout l'archet.
Whole bow-length.
Celým smyčcem.
Цѣлымъ смычкомъ.

*) Jede Variante auf dem ganzen Beispiel üben. | * On travaillera chaque variante sur tout l'exemple. | * Practice each variation throughout the whole exam]
* Každou změnu cvič na celém příkladě. | * Каждый варіантъ играть на цѣломъ примѣрѣ

Veränderungen in Achteln.

Variantes en croches.
Změny osminové.

Variations in quavers (eighth-notes).
Изменения восьмыми.

Mit einem Drittel des Bogens.
Avec un tiers de l'archet.
One third of bow-length.

Třetinou smyčce.
Одною третью смычка.

6

) Alle mit M bezeichneten Stricharten in der Mitte, an der Spitze und am Frosch üben.

) On travaillera les coups d'archet marqués de M du milieu, de la pointe et du talon.

) Practice the bowings marked M at the middle, tip, and frog.

) Všecky značkon M označené druhy smyků cvič ve středu, u hrotu a u žabky.

) Движенія смычка обозначенныя M исполнять срединою, концомъ и у колодочки.

B. & Cº 6128

13

B.& Cº 6128

(Coups d'archet 865-889)
(Bowing-styles 865 to 889)

(Coups d'archet 232-235)
(Bowing-styles 232 to 235)

B.& C? 6128

897*) Mit weniger Bogen, als bei Stricharten 232 - 235 angegeben ist.

897*) Avec moins d'archet, qu'il n'est indiqué aux coups d'archet 232-235.

897*) Use less bow-hair than in the bowing styles 232 to 235.

897*) Kratším tahem nežli při cvičeních smyč--cových 232-235.

897*) Короче, чѣмъ назначено при движеніяхъ смычка 232-235.

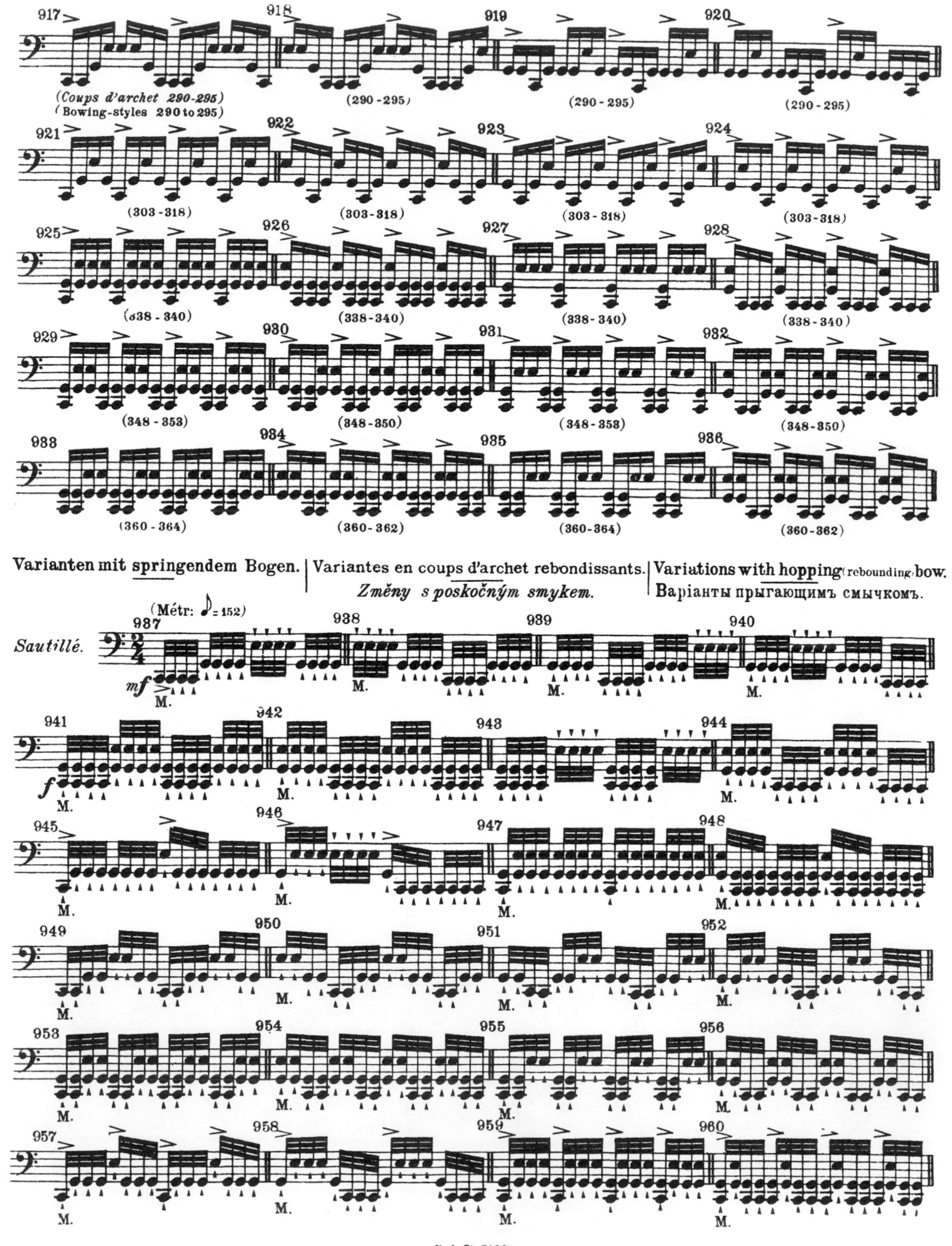